STARTING SCIENCE

ANIMALS

KAY DAVIES
AND
WENDY OLDFIELD

STECK-VAUGHN
LIBRARY
A Division of Steck-Vaughn Company

Austin, Texas

Starting Science

Books in the series

Animals
Electricity and Magnetism
Floating and Sinking
Food

Light
Sound and Music
Waste
Weather

About This Book

This book explores themes within the diversity of animal life and is concerned with both the similarities and differences that can be observed. It is intended to stimulate children's interest in themselves as humans as well as in the other creatures that share our world.

Animals provides an introduction to science inquiry methods. The activities and investigations are designed to be straightforward but fun, and can be used flexibly to suit the abilities of the children. Through them, the children use a variety of ways to explore the world around them.

The full-page picture in each chapter, with its commentary, may be taken as a focal point for further discussion or as an introduction to the topic. The theme and the animals looked at in each chapter can form a basis for more extensive topic work.

Teachers and parents will find that in using this book, they are reinforcing the other core subjects of language and mathematics. By means of its topical approach *Animals* covers many subjects usually taught in the early grades—exploration of science, the variety of life, the processes of life, genetics and evolution, and using light and electromagnetic radiation.

Editors: Cally Chambers, Susan Wilson

Typeset by Multifacit Graphics, Keyport, NJ
Printed in Italy by Rotolito Lombarda S.p.A., Milan
Bound in the U.S. by Lake Book, Melrose Park, IL
1 2 3 4 5 6 7 8 9 0 LB 96 95 94 93 92

Library of Congress
Cataloging-in-Publication Data

Davies, Kay.
  Animals / Kay Davies and Wendy Oldfield.
    p.   cm. -- (Starting science)
  Includes bibliographical references (p. 31) and index.
  Summary: Discusses animal life cycles, habitats, and physiology and examines physical similarities and differences in various species.
  ISBN 0-8114-3002-2
  1. Animals--Juvenile literature. 2. Zoology--Study and teaching--Activity programs--Juvenile literature.
  [1. Animals. 2 Zoology.] I. Oldfield, Wendy. II. Title.
  III. Series: Davies, Kay. Starting science.
  QL49.D36 1992   91-23413
  591--dc20   CIP AC

CONTENTS

Words that first appear in **bold** in the text
or captions are explained in the glossary.

Look at all the animals that live in our house.

ANIMALS

There are many different kinds of animals in the world.

What are the names of some that you know?

Find pictures of different kinds of animals. Put your animals in groups. Use the examples to help you.

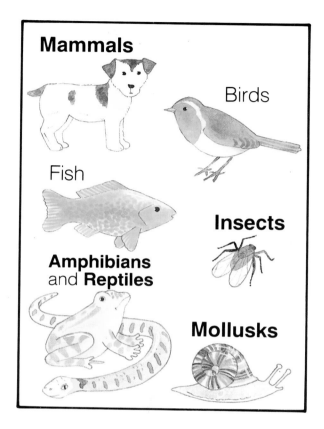

Mammals

Birds

Fish

Insects

Amphibians and **Reptiles**

Mollusks

Use your pictures to make an animal scrapbook.

Find out more about your animals. There are books about most of them in your library.

5

MY FAMILY AND ME

In some ways this boy looks like his parents. They all have black hair. The mother and father have brown eyes. But their son has blue eyes.

What color are your eyes? Are they the same as the rest of your family?

These twin brothers look exactly alike.

Find photographs of your family. Whom do you look most like?

Gather baby pictures with your friends. Can you guess who each baby is?

The foal looks like its mother and father.

Tadpoles are hatching from eggs. The tadpoles will live in the water until their legs have grown.

WHOSE BABY?

Tadpoles are baby frogs. But they do not look like frogs. They change as they grow.

In the spring, collect some **frog spawn**, or eggs, and watch how it changes. Keep it in a fish tank half-filled with pond water. Put in some pond plants. In one corner, pile up rocks higher than the water.

Make a tadpole diary. Check each change you see.

1		Black spot changes shape.	☐
2		Tadpole hatches.	☐
3		Back legs grow.	☐
4		Front legs grow.	☐
5		No tail. Frog hops out.	☐

Dogs have a very good sense of smell. These dogs can smell where the rabbits have been.

A GOOD NOSE

Test your own sense of smell. Ask a friend to fill some bowls with different things. Cover your eyes. Smell each dish and try to guess what is in it. Are there any that you can't smell at all?

Here are some animals' noses. Collect pictures of other animals with unusual noses.

Anteater   Horseshoe Bat   Crocodile

HOME OF MY OWN

Collect some snails. Pick them up gently—their shells break easily.

Put some folded wet newspaper at one end of a fish tank. Put dry newspaper at the other end. Place your snails in the middle of the tank. Watch where they go.

Snails like wet places.

Cut a small door in a cardboard box. Put your snails at the door. Which way do they go?

Snails like dark places.

Remember to put the snails back where you found them.

The snail carries its home on its back. When there is danger it tucks itself safely inside.

FINE FEATHERS

Look at these feathers. Some are long and some are fluffy.

The long feathers come from the wings and tails of birds. They are called flight feathers. They help the bird to fly.

The fluffy feathers are from birds' bodies. They help to keep the bird warm and dry.

Make a feather collection of your own.

A drop of water will run off a feather. Try this with a feather and see for yourself.

Look at ducks when they come out of the water. Watch how they shake the water from their feathers.

Some ducks are swimming on the lake. Other ducks are flying in the air.

The orangutan uses its long arms to swing through the trees.

A LONG REACH

Line up against a wall with your friends. See how high you can reach.

Ask someone to make a mark at the tips of your fingers.

Does the tallest person have the longest reach?

Can you reach to open the door, switch on the light, and ring the doorbell?

DON'T EAT ME!

Many birds eat butterflies. Some butterflies have spots on their wings that frighten the birds away.

Other butterflies are **camouflaged**. Their colors match the places where they live. They will not be eaten because they cannot be seen.

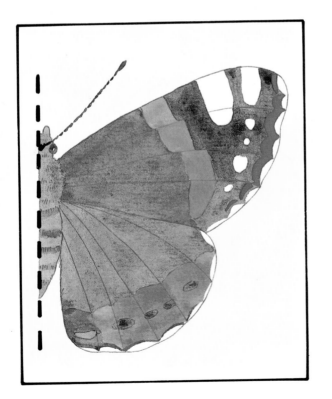

If you hold a mirror along the broken line you can see a whole butterfly.

Make your own butterfly.

Fold a large piece of paper in half. Paint half a butterfly on one side. Quickly fold the paper together and press hard. Open it up to see your butterfly.

18

Look at all the bright colors on the peacock butterfly's wings.
It is very easily seen.

There are many shells on the seashore. Some are broken and worn smooth by the waves.

SHELLS AND SHAPES

The shells come from animals that lived in the sea. Shells are very hard. They help to keep the animals' soft bodies safe inside.

Make a collection of shells. Are all of your shells the same color? Are their outsides rough or smooth?

Look at their shapes and put them into groups like this.

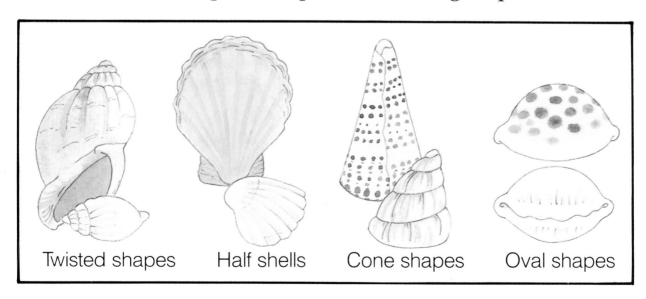

Twisted shapes   Half shells   Cone shapes   Oval shapes

Look and feel inside all your shells. The smooth surface helps the animal fit snugly inside.

The millipede has many legs. They move in waves down its body as it moves along.

LOTS OF LEGS

Look under stones, in holes, and in the soil for small animals like the millipede.

Look at their legs. How many do they have—six, eight, more, or none at all?

Carefully put the animals back where you found them.

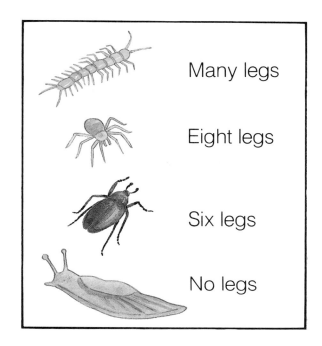

Many legs

Eight legs

Six legs

No legs

Make a small animal chart.

Get two paper plates and a fastener.

Draw pictures of your animals on one of the plates. Cut a V-shape out of the other plate. Use the fastener to pin the plates together at the center.

Slowly turn the chart to see what is hiding in the dark.

23

SHARP EYES

The cat's eyes face forward. This helps it to hunt.

The mouse's eyes are on each side of its head. It can look all around. It can see the cat creeping up on it.

Look at animals' eyes. Which animals are hunters and which animals are hunted?

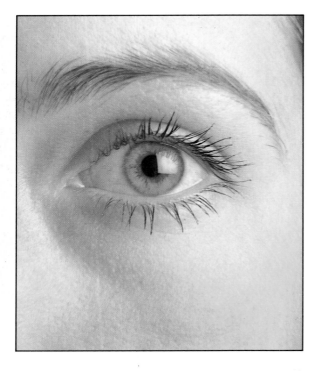

The colored part of an eye is called the iris. The dark part is called the pupil. The pupil lets light into the eye.

Find out the colors of your friends' eyes. How many have blue eyes? Brown? Green?

Owls can see well in the dark. They hunt for food at night.

The spider has spun a sticky web. It can trap a fly
for the spider to eat.

A STRONG WEB

People weave traps to catch food. Look at all the fish that have been caught in these nets.

You can weave a strong shape like the net.

Get two pieces of construction paper of the same size. Use two different colors.

Cut one into strips. Cut the other like a comb.

Weave your strips of paper in and out of the comb like this.

Can you think of some other ways that we use nets?

The chimpanzee is holding a stick in its hands. It can use the stick to dig for insects in the wood.

CLEVER HANDS

Chimpanzees' hands are a little like our own hands.
Our thumbs move toward our fingers. We can grip
things tightly with our hands.

Can you do all these things?

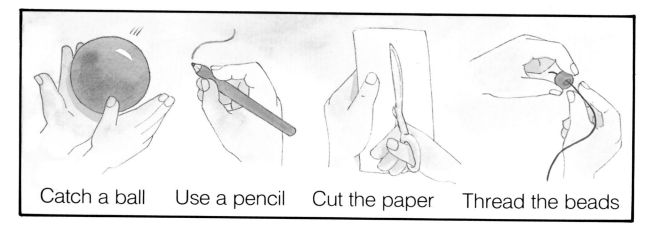

Catch a ball   Use a pencil   Cut the paper   Thread the beads

We can say things like this with our hands.

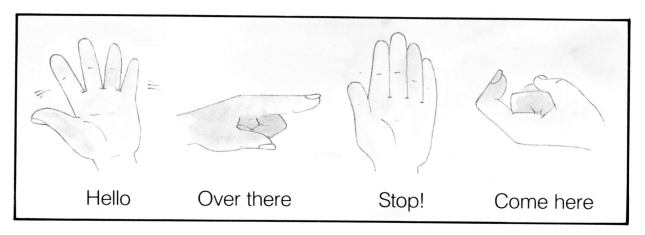

Hello   Over there   Stop!   Come here

How many more can you think of? Talk to your friends
with your hands.

GLOSSARY

Amphibians Animals that live in water and on land.

Camouflaged An animal is camouflaged when it is difficult to see because its coloring and pattern look like its surroundings.

Frog spawn The group of eggs from a frog.

Insects Animals with six legs.

Mammals Animals that feed their babies with milk.

Mollusks Animals that usually have a shell.

Reptiles Animals with scaly skin.

PICTURE ACKNOWLEDGMENTS

Bruce Coleman Ltd. 7 (Reinhard), 10 (Burton)), 13 (Burton), 19 (Purcell), 20 (Kahl), 22 (Clement), 24 (Freeman), 26 (Burton), 27 top (Cubitt), 28 (Davey); Chapel Studios (Zul Mukhida) cover, 4, 5, 6 top, 11, 12 both, 17, 21, 23, 27 bottom; Judith Court 9; Frank Lane Picture Agency 8 (Withers), 15 (Hamblin); Oxford Scientific Films 16 (Gibson), 18; Peter Stiles 14; Topham 6 bottom; ZEFA 25.
Artwork illustrations by Rebecca Archer. Cover design by Angela Hicks.

FINDING OUT MORE

Books to read:

All About Me by Melanie and Chris Rice (Doubleday, 1988)
Animal Footnotes by Q. L. Pearce (Silver Burdett Press, 1991)
Under the Sea from A to Z by Anne Doubilet (Crown, 1991)
The World of Animals by Tom Stacy (Random House, 1991)

The following series may also be useful:

Animals in the Wild (Raintree, 1986–87)
Animal Kingdom (Franklin Watts, 1986–88)
Animal World (Steck-Vaughn, 1990–91)
Eyewitness Juniors (Knopf, 1990–91)
First Sight (Gloucester Press, 1987–89)
Stopwatch (Silver Burdett Press, 1986–90)

INDEX

First published in 1990 by Wayland
(Publishers) Ltd.
©Copyright 1990 Wayland (Publishers) Ltd.